MISSA ASSUMPTA EST MARIA

FOR

SIX VOICES

BY

PALESTRINA

EDITED AND ARRANGED FOR MODERN USE BY

HENRY WASHINGTON

———

Duration of performance 30 minutes

———

CHESTER MUSIC LIMITED

PREFACE

THE only contemporary record of *Missa Assumpta est Maria* is contained in a manuscript copy dating from 1585-6 (Vatican Library—Capp. Sistina Cod. 76), which is at present inaccessible. Scheduled for expert restoration, it is said to be in so fragile a state that it cannot safely be handled or photographed. In the Breitkopf and Härtel Collected Edition of Palestrina's works, Haberl refers to this as the oldest and most genuine of available sources but does not claim to have transcribed it specifically for that edition.

Another manuscript, made in 1607 for the Duke of Altaemps, and now in the Vatican Library, is possibly no less genuine than the older copy. The scribe declares it to be a " most faithful transcription of the original," which " original " might well have been a Palestrina autograph, seeing that the appended *Christe eleison* for high voices is found in no other surviving source. From this copy (Ottob. Lat. 3386), Proske transcribed the Mass " with the greatest possible care " in 1835 for his collection *Musica Divina*. Our present edition is taken uncompromisingly from a microfilm of the same manuscript with corroborative detail from Capp. Sistina Cod. 137, the older of two eighteenth-century copies also in the Vatican Library.

In addition to the sources mentioned already there is a printed edition without date or printer's name in the library of Santa Maria sopra Minerva. Its origin remains uncertain though Haberl thought it might have been issued by the Medicean Press between 1612 and 1630. At any rate, this or another copy of the same impression may have inspired Baini's dramatic account of the Mass being hurriedly composed and rushed through the press in five days for a performance before Pope Sixtus V on the Feast of the Assumption, 1585. A note on the fly-leaf of Ottob. Lat. 3386 to the effect that the Mass had not been printed by 1611 serves to discredit yet another imaginative flight of Palestrina's ardent biographer.

Although no less than eighty of Palestrina's Masses were printed between 1554 and 1601—about half that number under the composer's direct supervision—*Missa Assumpta est Maria* was not among them. As the several Vatican manuscripts vary in many points of detail, the preparation of this new edition entailed prolonged research during which it became increasingly apparent that a definitive transcription was necessary. The first modern printed editions—Proske (1835) and Haberl (1888)—are often at variance: more recent editions—adapted possibly from the work of these great scholars—are hopelessly inaccurate. Thus, W. S. Rockstro produced an edition in 1885—owing an unacknowledged debt to Proske—in which note-values are freely altered to accommodate an arbitrary underlaying of the text. A well-known continental edition seems to have been engraved with Rockstro's version as copy, incorporating his false note-values, text-underlaying, numerous pauses and extravagant marks of expression. Even his engraver's omission of the words *Kyrie eleison* in the Bass part is faithfully reproduced. Reference to another model (probably Haberl) is indicated by amendments to the music text : a virtue outweighed by innumerable printing errors. Yet for half a ..ntury this corrupt version of *Missa Assumpta est Maria* has been the most accessible for quotation, study and performance.

Many nineteenth-century musicians have been justly criticised for revising Palestrina's works before reviving them. Nevertheless, Richard Wagner's treatment of the *Stabat Mater* is but a familiar example of a time-honoured custom observed by many of the Roman master's greatest admirers. It will suffice to recall that at the end of the sixteenth century a number of his compositions were reprinted with a *basso continuo* to bring them into line with the revival of accompanied liturgical song ; that Giovanni Anerio and Francesco Soriano both published arrangements of the six-part *Missa Papae Marcelli*, the one for four voices, the other for eight ; and that, a century later, J. S. Bach converted to a Lutheran *Missa Brevis* the *Kyrie* and *Gloria* from the six-part *Missa Sine Nomine*, adding an instrumental accompaniment. It is, therefore, not surprising to discover that even in eighteenth-century Rome, where a Palestrina tradition is said to have continued unbroken to this day, there were some who felt that the master's work stood in need of improvement. In a manuscript copy of *Missa Assumpta est Maria* made for the Pontifical Chapel in 1768 (Capp. Sistina Cod. 137), the ' restorations ' take the form of simplifying decorative formulae characteristic of Palestrina's melody, and of re-adapting the original text-underlaying to obviate word-repetition within the phrase. This latter expedient results in the amended part carrying a different text from that of the remainder, a defect which the composer would have been at pains to avoid. Strangely enough, there is here no multiplication of accidentals—indeed, the copyist erred on the side of omission. For this reason I have not hesitated to accept the evidence of this later manuscript in the matter of chromatic alteration where the older source proved undecipherable.

Composed in the familiar style of *Missa parodia*, the *Assumpta est Maria* Mass derives its themes from those of Palestrina's own six-part motet of the same title which, in turn, is a paraphrase of a Gregorian antiphon. In his ingenious reworking of the borrowed motifs the composer discovers a profound spiritual affinity between the words of the motet and those of the Mass.* His art of dividing the voices antiphonally in ever-changing groups of three or four parts was never more effectively applied than in this masterpiece. Every permutation of high and low voices in their several registers seems to be exploited to produce an exhilarating succession of varied harmonic textures.

Written in the Mixolydian mode, this music lies rather high in the original pitch and is here transposed a whole tone lower. Any further transposition downward would threaten the intrinsic clarity and lightness of this most radiant of Palestrina Masses. A practical approach to sixteenth-century polyphony leads to the conviction that middle parts were originally sung by men who had no compunction about exercising the full natural range of the voice. Where the 'falsetto' prejudice is encountered choirmasters may resort to a judicious intermingling of Altos with Tenors.

In this edition the music text is set out unencumbered with arbitrary marks of expression. Thus, while the director is free to insert such guides to performance as he thinks expedient, singers are spared the confusion induced by his insistence on a pianissimo reading when the edited score demands a contrary effect. The needs of inexperienced choirs have been met by incorporating a suggested scheme of interpretation in the *reductio partiturae*. It will be appreciated that the compression of six freely-crossing parts into a system of two staves precludes anything more than the broadest indications. The sign ˈ a short vertical stroke placed above or below a note, is freely used in this edition with the twofold object of defending verbal rhythm against the accentual power associated with the modern bar-line, and of defining the true agogic rhythm where an original long note has been replaced by two tied notes of shorter duration. Sixteenth-century note-values have been halved to accord with later acceptance of the crotchet as the normal unit of time, except for the ternary rhythm of the *Hosanna* in the *Benedictus* where the crotchet stands for an original semibreve. The slur is used solely to denote a ligature.

In underlaying the verbal text I have followed closely any indications implied in the Altaemps manuscript, while respecting the rules formulated by Żarlino and Vicentino in the sixteenth century. This apart, certain divergencies in the transcriptions of Proske and Haberl are referred to in foot-notes. In addition to these, Proske omits a number of ligatures and accidentals discernible in his source, though many of its recto pages are heavily blurred and the sharp sign is always excessively finely drawn. Haberl omits a few ligatures, chiefly in final cadences, but introduces a number of full accidentals which do not appear in either Cod. 3386 or Cod. 137. These are, for the most part, implicit in the style, and are incorporated in the present edition (with but one exception : p. 49, bar 4, Tenor 1) as part of the scheme of superscript accidentals which represents a sparing application of the theory of *musica ficta*. Haberl also presents an occasional re-arrange-ment of note-values, altering the rhythm without detriment to the harmony. Less defensible is his attempt to convert a free imitation into a strict one (p. 17, bar 84, Cantus 2), thus committing Palestrina to a breach of contrapuntal law. Even though it should transpire that the inaccessible Codex 76 provided the authority, the apparent licence could only be explained as a copyist's error.

Henry Washington.

The Oratory,
     London.
         April, 1956.

*J. Samson discusses this feature in his book : *Palestrina ou la Poesie de l'exactitude* and, at greater length, in the *Bulletin de la Societe Palestrina* of April 1933.

MISSA ASSUMPTA EST MARIA

KYRIE

PALESTRINA
Edited by
HENRY WASHINGTON

CH 08788

2

CHRISTE ELEISON*

*Alternative setting page 54

6

* Haberl halves this note, commencing phrase on third beat of measure.

8

GLORIA

12

* Proske gives A.

14

60

16

*Haberl gives D. See Preface.

CREDO

22

* Proske omits the phrase *Deum de Deo*.

24

* Haberl gives G.

Soon the music has to go
out of print . . . .

34

SANCTUS

.... and more fine works
are lost from the repertoire.

36

*Haberl gives a note of two beats in both Cantus parts.

38

BENEDICTUS

41

42

AGNUS DEI I

46

*Haberl gives a note of two beats.

48

AGNUS DEI II

50

Soon the music has to go
out of print . . . .

CHRISTE ELEISON II

The Chester Books of Madrigals
Edited by Anthony G. Petti

The Chester Books of Madrigals offer an exciting collection of secular European madrigals, partsongs and rounds from the 16th and early 17th centuries, newly edited from early sources by Anthony G. Petti, who contributes copious historical notes to each volume.

The majority of the settings are for SATB, and simplified keyboard reductions with suggested tempi and dynamics are provided as a rehearsal aid or as a basis for a continuo part where appropriate. Texts are in the original languages, English, French, German, Italian and Spanish, with modernised spelling and punctuation. In the case of the non-English texts translations are provided at the head of each piece.

An important feature of this anthology is the arrangement by subjects. which, it is hoped, should be of great assistance in programme planning. Indispensable popular works are interspersed with relatively unfamiliar but attractive and singable pieces.

Book 1: THE ANIMAL KINGDOM

1.	Jacob Arcadelt	*Il Bianco e Dolce Cigno*	SATB
2.	Adriano Banchieri	*Contrapunto Bestiale*	SSATB
3.	Orlando Gibbons	*The Silver Swan*	SAATB
4.	Josquin des Près	*El Grillo*	SATB
5.	Orlandus Lassus	*Audite Nova*	SATB
6.	Claude Le Jeune	*Petite Importune Mouche*	SAT: SSATB
7.	Lorenz Lemlin	*Der Gutzgauch*	SSSATB
8.	Claude Le Jeune	*Une Puce*	SATB
9.	Claudio Monteverdi	*Dolcissimo Usignolo*	SSATB; solo ad lib.
10.	Pierre Passereau	*Il est Bel et Bon*	SATB
11.	Thomas Ravenscroft	*The Three Ravens*	SATB; solo ad lib.
12.	Thomas Weelkes	*The Ape, the Monkey and Baboon*	SABar.
13.	Thomas Ravenscroft	Rounds from *Pammelia:*	
		(i) *New Oysters*	3 voices
		(ii) *The White Hen*	4 voices
		(iii) *The Old Dog*	3 voices
		(iv) *As I Me Walked*	4 voices
		(v) *Lady, Come Down and See*	4 voices
14.	Seventeenth Century Rounds:		
	(i) Anon.	*Well Rung, Tom*	4 voices
	(ii) Matthew White	*My Dame Hath a Lame Tame Crane*	4 voices
	(iii) Michael Wise	*A Catch on the Midnight Cats*	3 voices

Book 2: LOVE AND MARRIAGE

Love and Courtship

1.	Anonymous	*Mon Coeur Se Recommande A Vous*	SATB
2.	John Dowland	*Come Again*	SATB
3.	Melchior Franck	*So Wünsch Ich Ihr*	SATB
4.	Juan del Encina	*Mas Vale Trocar*	SATB
5.	Don Carlo Gesualdo	*Sospirava Il Mio Core*	SSATB
6.	Claudio Monteverdi	*Baci Soavi E Cari*	SSATB

Nuptials and Married Life

7.	Charles Tessier	*Au Joli Bois*	SATB
8.	Thomas Vautor	*Mother, I Will Have A Husband*	SSATB
9.	Thomas Morley	*Arise, Get Up, My Dear*	SAT
10.	Thomas Ravenscroft	*Leave Off, Hymen*	SATB; solo ad lib.
11.	Luca Marenzio	*Scendi Dal Paradiso*	SSATB
12.	Orlandus Lassus	*Quand Mon Mari Vient De Dehors*	SATB

Rounds on Love and Marriage

13.	(i) Thomas Ravenscroft	*O My Love*	4 voices
	(ii) Thomas Ravenscroft	*I Lay With An Old Man*	4 voices
	(iii) Thomas Ravenscroft	*Hey Ho, What Shall I Say?*	9 voices
	(iv) Thomas Ravenscroft	*What Hap Had I?*	3 voices
	(v) William Lawes	*Whenever I Marry*	3 voices

In preparation: Book 3 : Desirable Women
                           Book 4 : The Seasons

CHESTER MUSIC